LITTLE

TAPAS

THE LITTLE BOOK OF TAPAS

Copyright © Summersdale Publishers Ltd, 2024

Text by Benjamin Benton

An Hachette UK Company
www.hachette.co.uk

Summersdale Publishers Ltd
Part of Octopus Publishing Group Limited
Carmelite House
50 Victoria Embankment
LONDON
EC4Y 0DZ
UK

www.summersdale.com

Printed and bound in China

ISBN: 978-1-83799-124-2

The
LITTLE BOOK OF
TAPAS

Rufus Cavendish

Contents

Introduction

Hello and welcome to *The Little Book of Tapas*, your one-stop guide to a tempting selection of every possible iteration of Spain's most iconic small plates. Feast your eyes and make your mouth water with this wonderful collection of recipes and facts about the cornucopia of tapas dishes available. It's not hard to see why tapas are so popular, and not just in Spain.

No doubt you've got a taste for tapas already. It's what tapas are so good at, after all – inviting you to have a taste, igniting your interest, encouraging you to stay a while, eating and drinking a little more. And, in that spirit, you'll discover everything the wonderful world of tapas has to offer, be it the history of tapas, how it is eaten in Spain, how you'll find it abroad, and also how you can make it yourself at home.

From *albóndigas* to *boquerones*, *gambas* to *patatas bravas*, no stone will be left unturned in the quest to furnish you with all the information you'll ever need about the most sociable way of eating in the world.

By the end of this book, whether you end up believing that it was King Alfonso "The Wise", Spanish workers in the Middle Ages, or an Andalucian innkeeper who first placed a sliver of irresistible *jamón* over a glass of sherry and referred to it as a *tapa* (or top), the truth is, there is nothing better when you stop for a cold drink on a hot Spanish evening than to receive a little – often complimentary – plate of something savoury and outright delicious.

No matter the origin of the story, this delightful custom has endured, and with it, ensured that the popularity of tapas has extended far and wide from its Andalucian birthplace, so that whether you're in London, Paris, Tokyo, Los Angeles or Seoul, you'll be sure to find a place serving tasty little Spanish dishes.

THE
WONDERFUL
WORLD
OF TAPAS

Prepare to explore the wonderful world of tapas! Woven into the core of Spanish culture, tapas have always been intended as light, tasty snacks to fuel travel between bars. As such, tapas are social dishes meant to be shared with your family, friends and loved ones, and are an essential part of any great night out in Spain.

You don't have to be Spanish or in Spain to enjoy tapas. So popular has this way of eating become that you can find tapas, or tapas-inspired dishes, on many restaurant menus around the world. In this chapter, you will learn everything there is to know about tapas to fuel you on your journey deeper into this traditional Spanish cuisine.

What are tapas?

Fundamentally, "tapas" is a Spanish term for an appetizer or snack, although the word "tapa" in Spanish translates quite literally as "top" – originally a little cover to sit on top of your glass to keep bugs from falling inside.

This custom is still alive and well in traditional tapas preparation and serving. If you've ever eaten tapas, you'll be familiar with your server telling you that they "recommend two to three tapas per person". In a traditional Spanish tapas bar, dishes tend to be served in small terracotta bowls, known as *cazuelas*, or on small plates that can happily perch on top of your glass if needed.

Due to how delicious so many of the classic tapas dishes are, the concept of tapas has developed around the world into a meal that can be enjoyed sitting around a table with family and friends for lunch or dinner. In Spain, however, tapas tend to be enjoyed as part of an early-evening "crawl" that takes in two, three, four or more of your favourite tapas bars as you amble your way to your dinner reservation, or on your way home for your evening meal.

The tapas can range from a few delicious nuts or olives, anchovies and slices of local jamón, through to any number of tasty toppings, treats and spreads placed on little pieces of bread; all the way to fully fledged cooked dishes of meatballs, prawns, soups and stews – served as always in little dishes for the purpose of sharing with your fellow drinkers and diners.

What is the origin of tapas?

It is most likely that tapas originated organically as a little "tapa", or covering, for people's drinks in a hot and humid country where lots of little bugs are intent on landing in your hard-won thirst-quencher. The tapa would have likely started out as just a piece of bread, which people then perhaps dipped in their drink and ate, or even just discarded. Over time, clever bar owners realized that people stay longer and drink more if you give them a tastier tapa as opposed to just a stale piece of bread.

That said, the better the story the more people become obsessed with the legend. One version is that a less than scrupulous bar owner in the sixteenth century realized he could mask the low quality of his wine by serving a morsel of strong cheese or ham alongside it. If there is any truth in this, then perhaps we can thank this guy for the extraordinary cheese and cured meats produced in Spain today, as well as for inventing a culinary and cultural movement!

The most common legend dates back to the thirteenth century and King Alfonso X of Castile who, while recovering from an illness, was advised by his doctor to eat only small amounts of food at a time in order to build his strength. It is said that the king enjoyed this way of eating so much that he prescribed it for the rest of his subjects as the way to eat for ever more.

Another version of this legend suggests that the inns of Castile were so notorious for their rowdy and drunken patrons that the king introduced small portions of food to be eaten alongside a drink, in order to help sober up his raucous subjects and ensure they ended the night in a much more civilized manner.

The final regal theory goes that a latter-day King Alfonso was passing through the delightful Andalusian city of Cádiz in the late nineteenth century. Cádiz is famous for its windy weather so, not wanting the monarch to get sand in his drink, the bar owner placed a piece of ham over the top of this glass to protect it. This tickled the king's fancy and when he ordered his next drink, he asked for it "with the cover", or tapa.

WHAT DO SPANISH KEYBOARDS SAY? TAPAS!

How was tapas traditionally served?

As the legend goes, tapas were traditionally served as a "cover" for a drink. Whether it was a slice of jamón or a piece of tomato-rubbed bread, the tapas would have been simple and designed to be large enough to cover a glass, but robust enough to be picked up with your hands and placed back on the glass between sips.

As tapas developed though, the ubiquitous Spanish cazuelas (terracotta casserole dishes that come in every possible size) would have been used to contain whatever tapas had been prepared. It is the cazuela that is still perhaps the most recognizable serving dish, even today.

As tapas' popularity grew, so did the scope of the dishes offered and what they were served in. Nowadays, you'll find tapas served as traditionally as described above, but also in a contemporary fashion more in keeping with fine dining. However served, the spirit is the same – and you can still use your hands to eat them.

What are the three types of tapas?

Tapas dishes can be loosely categorized into three styles:

Cosas de picar, which translates as "things to snack on", tend to be snacks and nibbles – such as crisps, nuts and olives – that can be found served with drinks in many cultures. As is common with much of Spanish tapas, these will rarely be run-of-the-mill plain nibbles. It is common to find marinated or stuffed olives, smoked or spiced nuts, slices of cured meats, pickled anchovies or good local cheese, such as Manchego.

Pinchos, also often seen written as pintxos and translated as "skewers", are tapas that are "spiked" with a skewer or toothpick, which has a practical use of holding the tapa together and also being a way of tracking the number of tapas each diner has enjoyed. Pinchos can be an individual item such as a prawn or meatball on a skewer, although often they are simply something delicious on top of a small piece of bread that is skewered to make it easier to eat. While pinchos are often part of a broader tapas offering, in northern Spain – and in the Basque Country in particular – many bars consider themselves solely pinchos bars.

And finally, *cazuelas*, literally translated as "casseroles", refers to the little terracotta dishes that the tapas would have traditionally been cooked in. These are often slightly larger portions of food that might come with multiple components or are served in a sauce.

What are the most popular tapas dishes in Spain?

As a country with seventeen distinct regions, each with its own varied cuisine and preferences, it is hard to generalize about the popularity of each tapas dish. However, there are a few that prove more universally popular than others.

Jamón serrano (ham from the sierra, or mountain range) is an umbrella term for all dry-cured jamón produced in Spain, although most precisely it refers to jamón produced from white and/or non-Iberian breeds of pig. This is one of the most popular tapas dishes throughout Spain, and is perhaps the most globally recognized food item from Spanish cuisine.

Tortilla (Spanish omelette) is an egg and potato omelette that delivers so much more than its simplicity suggests. As a tapa, it is often served in wedges or as a tiny individual tortilla, although it is so popular in Spain that most people do not limit its consumption to a tapas crawl alone.

Patatas bravas (spicy potatoes) consists of little fried potatoes usually tossed in a paprika-spiced tomato sauce. These are often ordered just as they are, but can also be found with other ingredients such as fried fish, baked chicken or chorizo.

Croquetas (croquettes) in Spain are a little different from the potato croquettes many of us might have tried before. Largely a bread-crumbed and fried béchamel sauce flavoured with ham, cheese or shrimp, the end result is a hot, crispy exterior and a soft, oozing centre that is very hard to ignore.

Pan con tomate (tomato on bread) is a simple tapas dish that will not fail to delight: grated tomato pressed into a slice of garlic-rubbed toasted bread and often drizzled with good-quality olive oil and a crunch of salt. It is the single most popular tapas dish in all of Spain.

What are the most popular tapas dishes in other parts of the world?

If you asked a member of the public to name the first food that springs to mind when referring to Spanish cuisine they would likely say "chorizo". If its prevalence on tapas menus globally is a reliable barometer of popularity, then it is clear that chorizo, in one form or another, is a vital ingredient in the most popular tapas dishes outside of Spain.

After chorizo, tortilla and sliced jamón might be considered pretenders to the throne. A Spaniard would likely tell you that the stodgy wedge of egg and potato you're being served in London, Paris, New York or Sydney is not in fact tortilla (though it is meant to be), but we love it all the same. Similarly, chains of dedicated jamón shops have been popping up for decades in towns and cities around the world, and this is similar proof of the enduring popularity of this salty ham outside of Spain.

Finally, honourable mention must be made for gazpacho, the only chilled soup most of us have heard of and a true success story of tapas around the world. While it is most often served in small portions as part of a tapas spread, its addictive deliciousness means that outside of Spain - and when the climate calls for it - many of us can be found eating enormous bowls of gazpacho, it's rich, cold and garlicky goodness lifting our spirit and cooling our core.

What are some misconceptions about tapas?

The truth is that in Spain, as we are discovering, tapas and the customs surrounding the eating of tapas vary hugely between regions, and you would have a very different experience in San Sebastián than you would in Jerez. That difference and diversity has led to a couple of common misconceptions about tapas.

The first is that tapas are eaten by Spaniards every day. They are not. And while tapas are considered the most popular food of Spain, it is not how most people eat most of the time. It is a treat, an excuse to go out and meet family and friends, sharing a drink and some nibbles. It is an occasional indulgence.

This leads us to the next misconception that people eat tapas at home. This is not very common in Spain; instead tapas tend to be eaten out and about in bars. In other parts of the world, however, it can be very enjoyable to have a tapas spread for your Friday-night supper.

And finally, tapas are free. They are not, or not always. In a few places nowadays (the region of Andalusia, for example, as well as León, Santiago, A Coruña, Madrid and Seville) tapas do remain a largely gratis part of having a drink in the evening, but that free food bonanza is just a fantasy throughout most of the country. While almost every bar in Spain will serve you something to snack on with your drink, more often than not that free snack is nothing more than a bowl of crisps, olives or a slice of cheese. Of course, most of the time anywhere in Spain tapas can be ordered from a menu (and paid for) like any other dish.

Why is tapas important in Spanish culture?

It's chicken and egg as to which came first: the culture of Spanish people, which means they love to eat in a tapas style; or the tapas style of eating, which has led to Spanish culture being what it is.

Tapas is about sharing and conversation. You share your little plates with the person you are talking to, and this is central to Spanish culture and the way Spaniards like to operate. Tapas is about movement and discovery; you rarely stay in one place all night, you want to continue the journey, try the next bar, discover what might be going on as you move from place to place.

Tapas is about family and friends, it's about being outside in your community, and supporting the local bars and businesses. All of these things are central to Spanish culture as a whole. So, is tapas important to Spanish culture? Or is Spanish culture important to tapas?

HOW LONG?

The longest tapas bar ever erected was
520.99 m (1,709 ft 3 in.) long and was
created by Makro Autoservicio Mayorista
in Seville, Spain, on 6 October 2018.

To achieve the world record, 300 Sevillian caterers
teamed up to serve more than 45,000 tapas,
forming a bar that stretched between the San
Telmo Bridge and the Triana Bridge in Seville.

Tapas across the Spanish regions

As in any country with a varied and diverse history, you'll find that culture, climate, produce and cuisine change from region to region in Spain, taking influences from its different historical periods and its traditional, as well as developing, cultures.

What this means for tapas in Spain is that it varies too. Alongside the classics available up and down the country, you'll also find regional favourites that reflect the local produce and climate, as well as the preferences of residents.

Spain is divided into 17 regions, so let's go on a whistle-stop tour and discover the tapas to be found in each one.

Andalusia

This sun-kissed, southern tip of the country may be one of the most quintessential and idyllic places to enjoy tapas in Spain. Almost year-round perfect weather and a laid-back attitude to life make Andalusia the perfect place for a tapas crawl. This is one of the last remaining regions in Spain that still believes in giving you a free tapa with every drink – so the good times can still come cheap down here.

With so much beautiful coastline, Andalusia specializes in possibly the best seafood tapas in Spain. Be it *pescaíto frito* (fried fish), *espetos* (grilled sardines), *salmorejo* (similar to gazpacho, but thicker and more garlicky) or *ajo blanco* (chilled almond soup), you'll be well looked after in Andalusia.

Aragón

Aragón is a hidden gem. Not as well-known as Andalusia, perhaps, but its regional capital Zaragoza is renowned throughout Spain for its tapas scene, where some of the oldest tapas bars in Spain stand side by side with a new wave of upstarts serving innovative, modern tapas.

It is this blend of old and new that often makes tapas in and around Aragón such an enticing proposition. You'll eat some of the best pork-based tapas in Spain here, and you must try *ternasco* (tender roast lamb marinated in a wine-based sauce). It's a meaty region, that's for sure, with the cured meats among the best in the country, and the *arbiello* and *longaniza* sausages are not to be missed.

The tapas in Aragón tend to be hearty, reminding visitors of great home cooking, but beware, the portions lean towards the larger *ración* rather than classic tapas, so go steady and don't over-order in the first sitting.

Asturias

Overshadowed by its neighbour the Basque Country and the bright lights of Bilbao, Asturias may not be on the typical tourist trail, but it is one of Spain's few remaining almost untouched regions. You will perhaps have heard of the towns Gijón and Oviedo, both of which have a charming, old-world feel.

It is here in the *sidrerías*, or traditional cider houses, that you'll see bartenders and locals alike pouring their drinks the traditional way (by holding the bottle above their head and allowing a long, steady stream to cascade from a great height), which plays a central role in the full foodie experience. It is no surprise, therefore, that *chorizo a la sidra* (chorizo cooked in that very same Asturian cider) is the most famous dish of the region.

Balearic Islands

Better known perhaps for their beautiful
beaches and alluring night life, the Balearic
Islands actually have an eclectic and long-standing
tradition of tapas, with the offering here leaning
towards the more exotic end of the spectrum.

Spend some time on the islands and you'll be sure to
sample *sobrasada*, a spreadable version of chorizo;
and the *Mahón* cheese from Menorca, which has been
made in the same way since 2000 BCE and is renowned
for its sweet and nutty taste. Unsurprisingly, you'll find
plenty of fish and seafood on the tapas menus here,
and if you're feeling brave you're in the right place
for some of the best *caracoles*, or snails, in Spain.

The Basque Country

While the Basque Country has more of a restaurant culture, the tapas (referred to as *pinchos*) are some of the best in Spain.

With such extraordinary produce and culinary skill in this part of the country, the variety of pinchos available can be overwhelming, so perhaps start with the simplest of them all: a *gilda* of olives, *guindilla* peppers and salted anchovies, all brought together on a toothpick for your delectation.

The region has wonderful fish and seafood from the Atlantic Ocean, particularly anchovies and salt cod, and some of the best-quality meat and dairy products in Spain.

Don't leave without trying the *mejillones tigres*, or tiger mussels, so named for their spicy, tomato-based sauce. And always look out for dishes cooked "*al chilindrón*", which means in a flavourful sauce of local red peppers, tomatoes, onions and garlic.

The Canary Islands

Before becoming a popular holiday destination, the Canary Islands were a crucial stop for Spanish sailors returning from the New World. Nowadays, the tapas here have influences from Latin America and Spain, as well as North Africa due to their location off its coast.

Much like the Basque Country, the Canary Islands use their own word to describe tapas – *enyesque* – and each island has its own unique cuisine and culture. One tapa you can't miss is *papas arrugadas con mojo*, which literally translates as "wrinkled potatoes" (boiled in their skins in salted water) covered in *mojo picón*, a Tabasco-like hot sauce. Similarly, look out for *lapas*, or grilled limpets, which are served drizzled with fresh and spicy *mojo verde*, a tangy green sauce made with coriander.

Finally, in order to experience some of the diversity of tapas here, try the breadth of croquetas on offer; it's not unusual to see fillings such as blue cheese, banana, beetroot, and chicken curry.

Cantabria

Cantabria's unspoiled coastline and lush green forests may not correspond to the typical image of Spain you're imagining, but this region is home to some of the heartiest tapas in Spain. Unlike the Basque Country, Cantabria hasn't bothered so much with the fine-dining trend, which means many tapas in the region stay true to their traditional roots.

Santander is the tapas fan's mecca in Cantabria, with one of the best routes of tapas bars in the country. Due to its verdant pastures, Cantabrian milk (and therefore cheese) is incredible, so try it whenever possible, looking out for *queso de nata* (a rich, creamy cheese) and *queso picón* (a blue cheese made with cow's, goat's and sheep's milks).

Once you've sampled the cheeses, try the freshest seafood in Spain, straight from the Cantabrian Sea. Boquerones, or preserved anchovy fillets (*anchoas del Cantábrico*), are the local favourite, but all of it will be super fresh and absolutely delicious.

Castile-La Mancha

This is Don Quixote country, all whitewashed windmills and open plains. Its position right in the heart of Spain means that its cuisine features influences from Andalusia in the south, Valencia in the east, and Madrid in the north. The big cheese here, excuse the pun, is Manchego, so you will see it regularly at your table.

While not always the case, tapas here often come free with your drink, but try to show some restraint and leave room for *pisto*, a humble Moorish vegetable stew, reminiscent of ratatouille.

The final thing to look out for is the *migas* (breadcrumbs). Much of the local cuisine, including the Manchego, comes from the local shepherds' need for food they can carry and eat while roaming the plains for weeks on end. Migas are very tasty breadcrumbs, often cooked in lard with garlic and bacon, and you'll find them scattered over many of the tasty morsels you eat in this region.

LA TOMATINA

Did you know that Spain hosts the world's biggest food fight? Every year in August in Buñol, a small town in Valencia, a tomato festival called La Tomatina sees 20,000 people come together to throw some 145 tonnes of tomatoes at one another. Why? Purely for entertainment, of course.

The festival has been going since around 1945 and started when some friends, gathered for a celebration, decided to have a food fight and started throwing tomatoes at each other. At the same time the following year they gathered again and repeated the tomato fight. Each year they came and the gathering grew.

Madrid

Spain's cosmopolitan capital is one of the best places in the country to explore tapas. As you'd expect from an international city, the new is as readily available as the traditional. Certain neighbourhoods, such as La Latina, are packed cheek by jowl with tapas bars. You can find anything you want here, but *gambas al ajillo* has its roots in Madrid, so try it to find out why a land-locked city has spawned one of the best seafood tapas in Spain.

You might assume Madrid's tapas scene would be glitzier than in other places, but you'll often get tapas free with your drink here. Many of the best places are also the best value, so seek out traditional taverns like Casa Amadeo and Sylkar, where builders and high-society Madrileños sit side by side, sampling the best that the city has to offer.

Castilla y León

There's no shortage of culinary delights in Castilla y León. Despite its proximity to cosmopolitan Madrid, the food here tends to verge more on the traditional. Cities like León, Salamanca and Segovia are packed with tapas bars, many of which still serve the tapas free with your drink.

Perhaps the big highlight here is the *morcilla de Burgos*, a black pudding-like blood and rice sausage that is much better than it sounds. And if you like your meat more... meaty, then we suspect that *torreznos* might be up your street. A regional delicacy, torreznos is pork belly that's marinated, dried, cut into strips, then fried in olive oil, which is exactly as good as it sounds.

Castilla y León is also home to some of Spain's highest-quality bread, so make sure you use it to soak up the delicious sauces left behind on your plate.

Catalonia

The Catalan people are passionate and fiercely independent, and this plays out in their tapas too. Catalonia's capital, Barcelona, is a pleasure ground for foodies, and while the tapas don't come free, they're certainly some of the highest-quality dishes in Spain.

It is here that you'll feast on the super-simple original tapas of pan con tomate, which you'll find at every turn. And don't miss the *bomba*, or "potato bombs", which could be seen as the local version of croquetas. Potatoes and beef mince deep-fried and topped with bravas sauce and alioli is a good way to refuel during a long day of wandering.

Here you'll also find Romesco sauce, a piquant tomato and almond sauce that elevates everything it touches; and try *zarzuela* if you see it – a close cousin of bouillabaisse, it is a rich fish stew that shows off the best of the region.

Extremadura

From Extremo del Duero, which literally means "the no man's land on the bank of the Duero river", you can journey for miles around here without seeing another soul. Perhaps the Cinderella to Andalusia's more obvious charms, Extremadura's rugged landscapes are practically untouched by mass tourism, yet are home to some of the best, most relaxed tapas bars you'll find.

With influence showing from neighbouring Portugal, cities like Cáceres and Mérida have a thriving tapas culture. If you only eat one thing in Extremadura, it will likely be jamón ibérico. While you'll find it all over Spain, the best jamón ibérico can be found down here, as Badajoz is the thriving centre of jamón production in Spain.

Paprika grows on a massive scale here too, and you'll encounter its smoky richness in plenty of tapas. Look out for quail as well, often simply grilled, as it is a local delicacy that you might not have tried elsewhere.

Galicia

Wild and rugged, Galicia's tapas scene is an absolute must. Here, the focus is very much on quality of tapas rather than breadth of choice. You will not be able to avoid *pulpo a feira* – or *pulpo a la Gallega* as it is known outside of Galicia – which is octopus, boiled to perfection and seasoned simply with olive oil, salt and paprika. This might now be one of the most popular tapas in Spain, but it is at its best here.

Other local delicacies not to miss include *pimientos de Padrón*, or Padrón peppers, which are a spice roulette and delicious to boot; and the classic Galician *empanada* (a savoury baked or fried pastry turnover), of which you'll struggle to eat only one.

La Rioja

La Rioja, which gives its name to the famous wine of the region, has much to offer when it comes to tapas. Influenced by Basque pinchos in the north, the capital Logroño is home to seemingly endless tapas bars, many of which specialize in just one specific tapa. Generally, this means you're eating the best of that dish, as the bar has perfected it over the generations.

The region's famous *piquillo* peppers are ubiquitous, often stuffed with something delicious and always very good, and you'll find plenty of lamb-based tapas here, often simply a perfectly grilled lamb chop. Where you'll find patatas bravas on menus across the rest of Spain, here it is *patatas a la Riojana*, or a stew of potatoes and the local chorizo (which has a smokier spice than other chorizos throughout the country) that graces every menu.

Murcia

Sandwiched between Andalusia and Valencia, Murcia boasts 250 km (155 mi) of coastline, is known as Europe's vegetable garden and has a perfect climate. There's no shortage of beautiful old plazas and terraces lined with bars serving some of the best tapas in Spain.

Due to the region's vegetable-growing reputation, you'll find some of the freshest tapas in Spain. It's a vegetarian's dream too – seek out *palitos de berenjena*, or crispy fried aubergine sticks. Aubergine is one of Murcia's most typical ingredients, and fried vegetables are a common tapa all over the region.

Here there are groves of oranges and almonds, large market gardens and rice fields, so look out for rice dishes like *arroz caldero*, and don't ignore the paella either. Finally, make sure you try the region's most notable tapa, *marinera* – a bread stick or very thin piece of toasted bread, piled high with Russian salad and topped with an anchovy.

Valencia

This sun-drenched region, the easternmost in Spain, has an idyllic Mediterranean climate and fun-loving bar culture. You will immediately notice the groups of locals crowded around tables loudly sharing plates of food and conversation.

Much like Murcia below it, Valencia is famous for its paella, which you'll no doubt sample, but it has plenty of tapas on offer too. As you'd imagine with miles of Mediterranean coastline, in Valencia it's all about the seafood. Big fat mussels, little *clóchinas* and *tellinas* (smaller and sweeter than regular mussels), cuttlefish and super-fresh anchovies are served everywhere, and *esgarraet*, a zingy salad made with salt cod, peppers and plenty of olive oil, is very much a local delicacy.

Navarra

A medieval Basque kingdom, Navarra has influences from France and the Basque Country, meaning it has a rich tradition of good gastronomy. Most will have heard of Navarra due to its capital Pamplona, where the annual San Fermin festival sees the running of the bulls.

Across the region, the culinary tradition has focused on the social aspect of enjoying long, leisurely meals with family and friends, but there is always a time and place for tapas too. In Navarra, much like its Basque neighbour, tapas are referred to as pinchos, and are considered a sacred right, with people meeting to eat them at all hours of the day and night.

Particularly popular are pinchos of spicy local *txistorra* sausage; sharp, buttery *Roncal* cheese made with sheep's milk; blood sausage; and cod *ajoarriero*, which translates as "mule driver's garlic".

WORLD TAPAS DAY

Did you know that every year on the third
Thursday in June World Tapas Day is celebrated
across the globe? While not an official holiday,
the celebration was first conjured up in 2016
by Spain's national tourist board, Turespaña, to
honour its most famous cuisine and to give the
rest of the world a chance to celebrate it too.

Spanish tapas around the world

Of course, tapas are a Spanish invention and are central to much of the culture and cuisine in Spain. However, like any food with a worldwide reputation, tapas have found their way across borders by air, land and sea. So be you in Lisbon, London or Los Angeles, you will be able to find tapas or make them at home. All of this begs the question: how is tapas different around the world?

According to Spanish travellers there are two places outside of Spain where you can find tapas to rival what they have back home.

In Porto, Portugal, *petiscos* is seen as Portuguese tapas. With Portugal bordering Spain it is no surprise that the countries might share some culinary similarities. Petiscos are often served between meals and tend to feature many dishes familiar to Spanish tapas (such as olives and *calamares*), while Portuguese additions include octopus salad, *alheira* or *chouriço* sausages, and fried garlic shrimp.

In Andorra, another country that shares a border with Spain, there is a clear fondness for Iberian ham and tortilla, and many of the tapas featuring Pyrenean trout or garlicky snails could easily be from Spain.

Outside of Spain, Portugal and Andorra, is it possible to find good tapas to rival the home-grown affair? There are plenty of international restaurant chains offering an approximation of dishes that you might find on tapas menus, and many of these are very delicious indeed. However, one challenge of finding tapas beyond Spain is in replicating the social and cultural elements of enjoying tapas. The *ramblas*, or walking around and having tapas, is such a specific Spanish concept. The climate suits this way of eating too, as does the culture of the siesta, eating dinner late and going out as a whole family.

Tapas-style eating around the world

While not strictly tapas in the real sense of the word, there are of course ways of eating and types of foods in other cultures around the world that offer a similar experience to Spanish tapas.

PETISCOS

The closest thing to tapas from outside of Spain is Portuguese petiscos, found most commonly in Porto and Lisbon, with their offerings of fried squid, garlicky grilled prawns, and bowls of olives and other snacks designed to be eaten while out and about.

CICCHETTI

Venetian *cicchetti* are small snacks or side dishes, typically served in traditional "bàcari", or taverns. Popular cicchetti include little sandwiches, plates of olives and other pickled or preserved vegetables, halved hard-boiled eggs, small servings of a combination of one or more seafood, meat and vegetable ingredients laid on top of a slice of bread or polenta, and even tiny servings of typical full-course plates.

MEZZE

Found in Greek, Turkish and Middle Eastern cultures, mezze are a selection of small dishes served generally as appetizers, but which may also be served as part of a multi-course meal or form a meal in itself. Much like tapas, mezze are often enjoyed alongside an alcoholic drink and are designed to be shared with family and friends. Typical dishes might include dips and pickles with bread, alongside small plates of grilled or stewed meat, fish and vegetables.

BORRELLEN

This popular Dutch custom is also a selection of snacks to be enjoyed alongside a drink. Typical foods as part of a *borrel* (a social gathering involving drinks) might be *bitterballen* (deep-fried meatballs), *kaasstengels* (deep-fried cheese sticks) and *borrelnootjes* (deep-fried nuts).

SMÖRGÅSBORD

Literally translated as "a table full of open sandwiches", this Swedish custom has come to encapsulate any buffet-style spread of snacks and appetizers. A typical spread might consist of different kinds of fish and seafood, with pickled herring, prawns, smoked mackerel, cured salmon and fish roe, often featuring meatballs, hard-boiled eggs and cold meats, such as salami, liver pâté, smoked ham and sausage, as well as pickles, onions and various mustards.

KAP KLAEM

A Thai custom meaning "drinking foods", *kap klaem* tend to be salty, chewy, crunchy, sour and/or spicy treats that cut through the alcohol consumed. The type of dishes offered vary from region to region, but there are few foods specifically defined as kap klaem, as most dishes can be turned into drinking foods by adjusting their seasoning and portion size.

TAPAS DELICACIES

There is a down-to-earth element to most tapas menus, but at the same time tapas have always been a place for creativity. So, what are the most unusual and expensive tapas? Well, *angulas*, or baby eels, cost upwards of £1,000 per kg and look and taste like "dead worms", and yet, they are a beloved speciality in the Basque Country. Also look out for *zarajos*, or lamb intestines wrapped into a lollipop. It is also worth knowing the word *criadillas*, or testicles, as these can crop up on tapas menus and it's worth knowing what you are getting yourself into before you order!

THE
BIG NAMES

Much like a confident dancer as they stride towards a heaving dance floor, every tapas bar has its signature move – that combination of flavours and ingredients that will make someone's taste-buds tingle and ensure they come back for more. It is for these signature tapas that a region, city, town or bar might become especially well known.

Of course, there are the big names that one would expect to see on any respectable tapas bar or menu – the tried-and-true classics that the local and international reputation of tapas is built upon – and in this chapter we will break these down and profile exactly what it is that each of these classics brings to the menu.

Pimientos de Padrón
(Padrón peppers)

These small green peppers are a tapas staple. Originally from Padrón, a province in Galicia, northern Spain, they are usually fried in olive oil until their skins blister and they soften and wilt, before being served with a good crunch of sea salt sprinkled on top.

The catch – or the appeal, depending on your perspective – is that with any good batch of Padrón peppers most are mild and sweet, but about one in ten of any crop develops a hot kick that packs quite the punch. It is this little game of Russian roulette that has led to their popularity in the tapas arena. In any group of friends, there will always be one who is seeking out the little firecracker and one who wants to avoid it at all costs, but both are loving the sweet charred pepper taste along the way.

One more factor that makes Padrón peppers a very welcome addition to a tapas spread is that the staples of the menu will often tend to be potatoes, bread, tomatoes, prawns and pork in various forms, with very little in the way of freshness and greenery to cut through all the richer tasty bites. As such, a little plate of Padrón peppers, served as above or sometimes raw, can be a very welcome sight indeed.

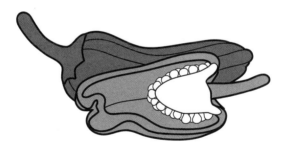

Croquetas (Croquettes)

Commonly made with ham (croquetas de jamón) although by no means limited to this, these little fritters are a favourite accompaniment to a cold drink.

Unlike croquettes in many other places, a Spanish croqueta eschews potato as its filling and instead uses a thick-set béchamel sauce to hold together any number of delicious ingredients before it gets breaded and deep fried. Other than jamón, other popular options you might encounter include spinach and cheese (croquetas de espinacas y queso), cheese (croquetas de queso), mushrooms (croquetas de boletus/champiñónes) and seafood (croquetas de marisco).

Albóndigas
(Spanish meatballs)

Almost every country in the world has a meatball, but few countries are so willing as Spain to experiment with them. If you trawl enough tapas bars and read enough menus you will likely find albóndigas of every flavour and hue, and almost each and every one will be more delicious than the last.

Derived from *al-bunduq*, the Arabic word for hazelnut (and by extension the word for a small round object), albóndigas are thought to have been imported to Spain during its period of Muslim rule. This perhaps explains the breadth of variety of albóndigas and why beef, lamb, fish, vegetables and poultry are used for albóndigas as much as pork.

Usually rolled a little smaller than your typical Swedish or Italian meatballs, albóndigas are served in a rich, often-garlicky tomato sauce, and are the perfect accompaniment to a good glass of Spanish red wine.

WHAT
A GREAT
WAY TAPAS
THE TIME!

Patatas bravas
(Spicy potatoes)

Spicy potatoes, indeed, patatas bravas are much more than the sum of their parts. Little more on paper than small cubes of fried potato topped or tossed with a rich spiced tomato sauce, the combination of hot potato and paprika-rich sauce somehow has the power to solve all ills and right a wayward evening.

One of the most ubiquitous tapas available, it is likely one of the first a child might try and one of the last a Spaniard might request when they want just one more bite of something.

While in Madrid patatas bravas are generally served just with the tomato sauce, across the country you will also often find aioli drizzled across the top to help cut through and balance the richness. Equally, a variety of other toppings can be ordered with the snack, such as chorizo slices or fried fish. As is often the case with most tapas, local or regional quirks and peccadillos are encouraged, and delicious new combinations and toppings discovered.

Calamares fritos
(Fried squid rings)

While you can travel to most hot countries with a coastline and have a very passable plate of fried squid, there is something magical about calamares fritos in Spain, and their ubiquitous sidekick aioli helps elevate them to a particularly pleasing experience.

This is helped by the thick batter so often employed in tapas bars, as well as whippet-quick frying in very hot oil, designed to ensure the squid is kept as tender as possible.

Always served with a wedge of lemon, often calamares fritos are the classic ring shape, although keep an eye out in Cantabria and the Basque Country, where the calamares might be described as *rabas* and are cut into straight strips. Also delicious and to be sought out are battered and fried baby squid, known as *puntillitas*.

Gambas al ajillo
(Garlic prawns)

Have you even had tapas if you've not had gambas al ajillo?

Fresh prawns cooked in a piquant garlicky olive oil might just be the perfect tapas. We all know instinctively that prawns and garlic go perfectly together, and it just so happens that they are a harmonious accompaniment to sherry, the true tapas professional's drink of choice. It also helps that the leftover oil at the bottom of the dish they're served in is the ideal sopping-up liquid for good Spanish bread.

The traditional preparation for gambas al ajillo is simple perfection: heat a glug of olive oil in an earthenware cazuela and add thin slivers of garlic to flavour the oil. Then add the fresh prawns and cook them ever so briefly before adding a splash of sherry vinegar to lift and finish the dish. That's it. All that remains is for you to pick through the prawns and separate the sweet fragrant flesh from the shells.

Jamón serrano (Serrano ham)

Jamón serrano (or ham from the sierra, or mountain range) is an umbrella term for this particular dry-cured style of ham. While jamón is very similar to Italian prosciutto or Portuguese *presunto*, it is the particular type of Spanish Iberico pig that the jamón is taken from that gives a good jamón serrano its distinctive depth of flavour.

The Iberian pig, or black pig, is distinctively black and has been bred for its wonderful flavour. This flavour is also enhanced further by the fact that the pigs exist largely on a diet of acorns and foraged treats that can be found on the oak forest floor.

A plate of good jamón serrano will have been carved from the preserved leg of an Iberian black pig. The leg will have been salted for two weeks, then washed and hung to dry for six to 18 months (depending on the size and climate) in order to develop a wonderfully deep and complex flavour that highlights all the nutty richness of the Iberico pig.

You will recognize the jamón as the big haunch of meat held in a vice-like contraption behind (or on) the bar in many tapas establishments. It is a real skill to perfectly carve sliver after sliver of wafer-thin jamón.

Pan con tomate or pa amb tomàquet (Bread and tomato)

Before we start any arguments, officially pan con tomate and *pa amb tomàquet* are two different things. Pan con tomate is Spanish and tends to be toasted bread rubbed with garlic and then topped with grated tomato, sometimes rubbed onto both sides, with oil and salt the only other adornments. As things that are greater than the sum of their parts go, this is symbiosis at its very finest.

The original form of this classic tapa comes from the Catalans and is known as pa amb tomàquet, or bread and tomato, and is made in exactly the same way as the more ubiquitous pan con tomate, but perhaps with added Catalan passion.

HOW MUCH FOR THAT JAMÓN?

Jamón is a national obsession in Spain, and the global popularity of tapas has no doubt made it one of the country's most successful exports. Eduardo Donato's rare variety of acorn-fed Iberian pigs produces the world's most expensive jamón. This jamón costs an eye-watering €4,100 (£3,600) a leg.

Tortilla
(Spanish omelette)

No, not the Mexican crunchy or soft kind that you use to spoon guacamole into your mouth or the casing of your burrito. Spanish tortilla is a potato, onion and egg omelette or frittata that is served at room temperature and, once again, is the purest form of culinary alchemy as it is very much more than the sum of its parts.

Made by cooking lots of sweet onion and cubes (or slices) of potato in oil until soft, sweet and unctuous, before pouring in plenty of beaten eggs and cooking slowly until only just set, a good Spanish tortilla will have a depth of savoury flavour that is unparalleled.

A stalwart of any tapas bar, it is also a sure-fire way to tell the quality of the establishment you are visiting – overly set in the middle or under-seasoned and you know the rest of the menu won't be much to write home about either. Many people in Spain have their favourite spot for tortilla, and they are not always the most salubrious.

Often it might be the tortilla in a service station, or in a run-down bar, or even in an unsuspecting corner shop that does it for you.

Boquerones en vinagre
(Pickled anchovies)

The central ingredient of the dish is the boquerones, or fresh anchovies, which initially have a brown-coloured flesh, much like a typical anchovy used in regular cooking. However, in this instance they are cleaned, de-scaled and submerged in either a salt water bath for 3 hours and then vinegar for 6 hours, or a 3:1 mix of vinegar and olive oil, already seasoned with garlic, parsley and salt for two days.

During both processes, the fillets slowly turn white as the vinegar reacts with the flesh. Once processed and the liquid has been drained, the boquerones are seasoned with garlic, olive oil and parsley to become the piquant little slivers we are presented with.

Boquerones are served cold and usually with beer or a soft drink rather than wine or sherry as their vinegary nature can slightly jar with wine. The dish is especially popular during the hottest summer months and is often accompanied by potato chips.

Gildas (Skewered anchovies, olives and hot peppers)

If you're ever asked which tapa was named after a character in a movie, gilda is the answer.

Invented only 65 years ago in San Sebastián, gilda is so named as the eponymous film was pretty risqué but managed to slip through the censors' net during Franco's rather draconian rule of Spain. During a tough period for the country, the film inspired locals to create a spicy pintxo as a subversive endorsement of the character's boldness and independence.

All these years later, Rita Hayworth posters remain popular in the wine bars of San Sebastián as an homage, as do small glass jars filled with these skewered stacks of Manzanilla olives, guindilla peppers and anchovies. Gildas have become internationally popular, their subtle spiciness and bright flavour making them a perfect partner for a cocktail or glass of wine, sherry or cold vermouth.

Pinchitos (Skewers)

Pinchitos or *pinchos morunos* are skewered pieces of meat, generally grilled over charcoal. A welcome upside of the Moorish occupation of Spain back in the day, these have understandably stood the test of time and are now a firm fixture on all tapas menus.

The name pinchitos is used in the south of Spain, specifically Andalusia and Extremadura, but you'll find them referred to as pinchitos or pinchos morunos all over the country.

Pinchitos are usually made using cubes of pork or chicken, and are marinated with olive oil and spices, generally a heady mix of garlic with any combination of cumin, thyme, paprika, oregano, turmeric and pepper, many of which reflect the Moorish influence of their invention.

Unlike most tapas that are only really cooked, served and eaten in tapas bars, pinchitos are often the main meat dish cooked at Andalusian and Extremaduran barbecues during the summer months.

Montaditos
(Tiny sandwiches)

Dating back to the fifteenth century and the very first occurrence of a sandwich in Spain, *montaditos* are the Spanish version of an open sandwich. They are similar in construction to those you might find in Scandinavia, or even an Italian bruschetta, but with a much looser attitude to toppings and almost no limitation as to what should or shouldn't be collected on top of the little pieces of bread that serve as a canvas for the montadito artist in each tapas bar.

The name montadito is believed to stem from the word *montar*, meaning to mount – as a reference to all the toppings piled on top of each bread slice. The toppings themselves may include any combination of smoked meat, chorizo, jamón, cheese, pickled vegetables, anchovies or any other type of meat, seafood or delicious ingredient that might just be to hand. The combinations are endless and, with no rules, vary wildly from bar to bar.

Chorizo (Spicy sausage)

A sausage with a heady mixture of chopped pork meat, pork fat, salt, whole peppercorns, cinnamon, achiote and other spices, chorizo is perhaps the best-known Spanish ingredient worldwide and a tapas stalwart to boot.

While outside of Spain we are most used to a cured chorizo that can be sliced and eaten straight away, most applications of chorizo on a tapas menu use the raw version that is grilled and served as it is, or cooked in a vinegar- or tomato-based sauce, all the better to draw the salty, porky, paprika-rich oil from the sausages and leave a sauce crying out to be mopped up with plenty of good Spanish bread.

FIESTA DEL AGUA Y EL JAMÓN (THE WATER AND HAM FESTIVAL)

Perhaps Spain's most unusual food festival, this is held in the village of Lanjarón near the city of Granada, which is known for its mineral water and local ham. As such, on the Noche de San Juan (the Night of Saint John) on the 23 June every year, the village hosts a giant water fight at midnight, after which it's time for feasting on slices of local ham.

HOW TO
EAT TAPAS

It should be clear by now that there are almost no rules for what tapas are, or can be, nor how they should be eaten. As such, you do you. That said, generally tapas are designed to be shared, so there should be several per portion.

They're also designed to be eaten with toothpicks, although they can just as often be small individual dishes with their own cutlery, and equally it is perfectly acceptable to eat tapas with your hands. Standing up outside a bar or sitting around a table, be ready to share and prepare to lick your fingers, because eating tapas is about as relaxed a way to eat as you'll find anywhere in the world.

Typical tapas foods

Typically, good-quality local ingredients are used to make tapas. At their most traditional, you might find local meat, cheese, vegetable or seafood cooked or marinated and placed on slices of local bread. Local nuts and olives also feature prominently in most tapas spreads. If the region you're in happens to have a long coastline, then seafood will feature heavily, and if the land around you is used for farming, then the vegetables, wheat, livestock and dairy of that area will no doubt be on the menu.

It would be rare to find a tapas menu that didn't have at least one tapa of prawns, anchovies, chorizo, jamón, tomatoes or peppers in some variation of deliciousness on it, but seeing as very few rules apply to tapas – and the Spanish are a creative and ingenious people – you will find almost anything delicious thrown in the mix when the moment takes them.

When it comes to key flavours and seasoning, you will find garlic, paprika, olive oil, lemon juice and vinegar in almost all tapas recipes.

How are tapas presented?

How your tapas are presented tends to depend on the type of tapas being served.

At one end of the spectrum nuts, olives and crisps tend to be served in little bowls or more traditionally small terracotta cazuelas.

If you're ordering montaditos or other pinchos, these will usually be skewered or served with toothpicks and brought to you on little plates, in cazuelas or sometimes on a slate.

Hot tapas, be they Padrón peppers, something fried, a stew, or anything in between, will tend to be served on a plate or cazuela and will be accompanied by toothpicks, cutlery or napkins, depending on what makes most sense.

Apart from the plates, the most common elements of tapas presentation will be the napkins and toothpicks that are so necessary when eating.

Tapas time

A tapa was traditionally something to enjoy with a drink to whet your appetite before having lunch or dinner at home, and not much has changed.

When you meet somebody for tapas in Spain, that usually means a drink and a bite to eat. Having tapas for lunch would see you sit down between 2 p.m. and 3.30 p.m., while dinner usually starts at around 8.30 p.m. and can merrily go on until midnight.

You might be tempted otherwise, but sticking to these times will ensure you get the freshest food and the best atmosphere, which is what tapas are all about after all.

Where should you eat tapas?

Tapas bars are usually exactly that – bars or taverns – rather than cafés or restaurants, and in most towns and cities the best tapas bars tend to be surrounded by other good tapas bars, all of which helps facilitate the customary tapas crawl. As an outsider it can be hard at first glance to know the best places to go to, but do your research – use the internet, guidebooks or ask locals and staff – and you can't go wrong. It is important to remember that tapas are almost always served in bars as opposed to restaurants – a restaurant serving a tapas menu is likely to be touristy and less authentic.

One top tip if you're following your nose on the hunt for tapas: the best bars are likely the ones that fill up fast as the locals in the know pack into their favourite haunts, so anywhere already heaving by 1.30 p.m. or 8.30 p.m. (the start of lunchtime and evening tapas) is likely a local favourite and the one you should try. Many bars are standing-room only, so expect to eat on your feet at the bar or at a high table.

Tapas tips

When seeking out tapas somewhere for the first time, order a drink and see what is brought with it. In many places you might get a different tapa each time you order, in other places you might not get anything at all, but at least you will know where you stand. If the tapas have arrived with your drink without you ordering any food, this is the sign that they're complimentary.

Tapas should be taken standing, usually at the bar. This action of eating small quantities while standing is referred to as *picar* (pecking) as opposed to *comer* (eating).

Another tip that locals live by is not to eat more than two tapas at any one place. The idea behind *ir de tapas* (literally translated as "to go for tapas") is to eat a little and move on to the next bar.

And finally, learn to combine the right tapas. For example, a little plate of gambas (prawns) would go nicely with one of pulpo (octopus) but may not complement caracoles (snails) quite as well.

USEFUL PHRASES

¿Me da [...], por favor?
Could I have [...], please?

Una tapa/un pincho de [...].
A small portion of [...].

Una ración de [...].
A meal-sized serving of [...].

¡Salud!
Cheers!

La cuenta, por favor.
The bill, please.

How many dishes should you order?

In terms of how much to order, as a rule of thumb the "pinchos" are individual and anything that comes plated is usually a "ración" designed to be shared. Allow one pintxo and one ración per person in your group, assuming you'll also be given some nibbles and some bread.

For four people you could order a pintxo each initially, before ordering four raciónes to share. When selecting raciónes, a Spaniard would always aim for a mix of styles and ingredients – for example, something cold, something grilled, something fried and a stew, and these might be one meat, one fish, one vegetable and a wild card, perhaps something unusual or the speciality of the bar or region.

When Spaniards meet for tapas, they will usually order pinchos while they are standing at a crowded bar, and will move onto raciónes once they can find a table or a bit more space.

If you are eating alone, you can stick to ordering pinchos, which are perfect for one, or you can definitely ask for half raciónes as most places are now happy to do this.

If you're not sure what something is, just ask. The Spaniards take great pride in the creativity of their tapas and will be happy to answer any questions.

Make it clear if it's a tapa you're after (a mini portion) or a ración (a meal-sized serving), or you'll end up paying a lot more than you planned.

Tapas etiquette

As with any centuries-old custom central to a country's food culture, there are plenty of rules and etiquette that are followed in the preparation, ordering and cooking of tapas and yet, at the same time, there are no rules at all.

Having said that, there are certainly some guidelines worth noting before diving head first into a tapas crawl and, as with anything in life, in order to break the rules it is useful to know them in the first place.

The rule followed almost religiously is that all food is ordered to share and no dishes are exclusively for one person. With this in mind, as each plate is a communal treat for the table, a basic courtesy to follow is that no double dipping is allowed.

You'll also need to use your fingers, a lot. Often skewers, toothpicks or an individual fork are provided, but knives are not needed and rarely given, so very often you'll receive a few plates of tasty treats already divided into individual portions, a stack of napkins and nothing else. This is a joyful way to eat, and using your fingers to pop something into your mouth before greedily licking them clean is very much a legitimate approach.

In very busy tapas bars feel free to shout for your order, even waving your arms in the air to get the waiter's attention. Often, the waiters expect it and you might be ignored if you opt for a more timid approach. There is a Spanish phrase that translates loosely as "leave your manners at the door and collect them when you exit", and it is in this spirit that you'll notice many people in a traditional tapas bar behave.

MAKING
TAPAS

While tapas are often enjoyed as they were invented, out on the street, with each tapa a partner for a drink, it is a shame to consign them to something you can't make yourself. After all, most tapas are very easy to recreate at home and lend themselves perfectly to cooking for one person or catering for a crowd. There's no reason why you should miss out on these delicious treats just because you don't live in Spain or anywhere near a tapas bar.

What follows are recipes to recreate that authentic experience from the comfort of your own kitchen. These dishes are as fun to make as they are to eat, are simple yet delicious, and can be enjoyed with family and friends, or you can keep them all for yourself.

Key equipment

Before you embark on any of the recipes that follow, let's make sure you have everything you need to pull off each one with relative ease.

ESSENTIALS
- Chopping board
- Sharp knife
- Frying pan
- Saucepan
- Skewers (metal or bamboo)
- Mixing bowls

OPTIONAL
- Griddle pan or outside grill
- Cazuelas, or little terracotta bowls of varying sizes
- Pestle and mortar (for sauces and spices)
- Toothpicks

Key ingredients

Little is set in stone when it comes to making tapas, and for almost all of the following recipes you should feel free to substitute one ingredient for another, depending on what you like and what you have in your cupboard or fridge. That said, if you tend to always have the following key ingredients at home, then you'll be set up and ready to go whenever the urge to make tapas takes you.

CHORIZO

A fully dry-cured chorizo can be eaten without cooking and is almost indestructible if stored in a cool dry place. You'll find *picante* (hot) or *dulce* (mild and sweet) chorizo in most good food shops, and they can be used interchangeably to suit your tastes. Some tapas recipes call for fresh chorizo, which should be kept in a fridge and needs cooking – this sausage is shorter and is presented as a string of sausages. Many speciality food shops will have them in stock.

CHEESE

While Spain produces a variety of cheeses, Manchego is the one we all tend to know and love. Any hard cheese can be used in its place, so use what you have, but if you can buy some nice Manchego, then why not treat yourself.

TOMATOES

When in season, a good ripe tomato should always be in your larder; and when out of season, always have cans of good-quality plum tomatoes to hand.

PEPPERS

Be they green, yellow or red, peppers are essential in many tapas recipes.

ONIONS

Purists would suggest specific onions for specific recipes, but just use whatever you've got.

GARLIC

Almost unavoidable in many tapas recipes and one of the main reasons tapas are so delicious.

CHILLIES

A fresh red or green chilli (or some dried red chilli flakes) can easily up the heat of your tapas dishes.

ALMONDS

Often, crushed almonds are used to thicken sauces, or in the case of Romesco sauce and ajo blanco are a key ingredient in their own right.

OLIVE OIL

Perhaps the most important ingredient in all tapas dishes. The oil you use should be extra virgin, or from the first press of the olives.

PAPRIKA

Made from ground dried red peppers and often found as sweet smoked or hot smoked, paprika is used liberally in many classic tapas dishes.

PARSLEY

Possibly the most widely used herb in tapas. Oregano, basil, bay leaves and thyme will also come in handy.

Key techniques

FRYING

In this instance, we're talking generally about deep-fat frying (i.e. completely immersing food in hot oil), although in a home kitchen you can shallow-fry instead (turn regularly to achieve a deep-fried effect) to achieve the same results. In order to deep-fat fry at home you'll need a large high-sided saucepan and a thermometer, or you could invest in a counter-top deep-fat fryer if you see yourself making a long-term commitment to making croquetas or patatas bravas at home.

GRILLING

Plenty of tapas dishes call for something tasty such as a prawn, chorizo or squid to be grilled hard and fast over high heat. In a typical tapas bar this would be done on a large cast-iron flat plate called a *plancha*, but at home you can use a griddle pan, an outside grill or barbecue, or even a good frying pan. You'll need to feel comfortable cooking over high heat, and will want to make sure you have good extraction or are able to open a window as quite often things can get a little smoky.

STEWING

Quite often a larger tapas dish might call for a slow-cooked sauce or be a stew, such as chorizo in cider or squid cooked in its own ink. In this instance, you'll be called to cook off ingredients over a medium or high heat before reducing the heat, and letting things blip away until soft and cooked.

BLENDING

Plenty of tapas recipes call for a sauce such as bravas, romesco or even aioli to be made as part of the end dish. In this instance, you'll either have to whip out the blender or, if you're more of a purist, find a pestle and mortar and slowly grind a sauce into existence, which is hard work but somehow often more rewarding and delicious.

Measurements

The recipes in this chapter use metric measurements, but if you prefer using imperial (and you don't have a smartphone to do the conversions for you), here are some basic tables:

25 g ≈ 1 oz	15 ml ≈ ½ fl. oz
60 g ≈ 2 oz	30 ml ≈ 1 fl. oz
85 g ≈ 3 oz	75 ml ≈ 2½ fl. oz
115 g ≈ 4 oz	120 ml ≈ 4 fl. oz
255 g ≈ 9 oz	270 ml ≈ 9 fl. oz

Making tapas

TAPAS
RECIPES

Aioli (Garlic mayonnaise)

This piquant garlicky sauce is often responsible for elevating a simple tapa to legendary status. As such, we simply have to show you how to make it at home.

Serves 4

INGREDIENTS

4 garlic cloves, peeled and sliced
½ tsp coarse sea salt
Juice of ½ lemon
120 ml olive oil

METHOD

In an ideal world, you'll make this with a pestle and mortar: the grinding of the garlic is what allows the sauce to take on a mayonnaise-like consistency. If your kitchen is without, use a blender instead.

Place the garlic and salt in the mortar or blender. Mash with a pestle or blend to a fine paste, working the garlic and salt together for 4–5 minutes. Add the lemon juice and mix to combine.

Next, add the olive oil little by little, grinding or blending until completely incorporated between each addition. Continue incorporating the oil until the aioli thickens up and starts to look creamy. If the aioli gets thicker than you'd like, add a few drops of cold water and grind or blend it in to loosen.

Aioli is best eaten fresh, but will keep for 24 hours in an airtight container in the fridge.

Pimientos de Padrón (Padrón peppers)

If you can find Padrón peppers locally, this is how to prepare them exactly as you would find them in any tapas bar in Spain.

Serves 4

INGREDIENTS

1 tbsp olive oil
500 g Padrón peppers
Pinch of coarse sea salt

METHOD

Heat the olive oil in a large frying pan over a high heat. Put the peppers into the pan and shake the pan so they settle into a single layer. Fry the peppers, tossing or stirring frequently, for 5 minutes until blistered, blackened and soft.

Transfer the peppers to a serving plate or bowl and season with the sea salt.

Pimientos del piquillo (Stuffed piquillo peppers)

Typically, these peppers are stuffed with tuna, goat's cheese, salt cod or crab, but the options are generally limitless.

Serves 4

INGREDIENTS

200 g mayonnaise
145 g tin tuna, drained
Juice of ½ lemon
4 tbsp olive oil
¼ tsp coarse sea salt

Small handful of parsley, roughly chopped
1 jar of roasted piquillo peppers or 12 preserved red peppers, drained

METHOD

Combine the mayonnaise, tuna, lemon juice, olive oil, salt and parsley. Using a teaspoon, stuff this mixture into each of the drained piquillo peppers.

They can be served as they are, on top of toasted bread, or baked for 10 minutes and enjoyed alongside potatoes or rice.

Pan con tomate
(Tomato on bread)

It doesn't come much simpler than tomato on bread, but nor does it get much more delicious. Use good tomatoes and this will taste better than you could ever imagine.

Serves 4

INGREDIENTS

1 baguette
1 garlic clove, peeled and halved
Olive oil
2–3 tomatoes
Pinch of fine sea salt
Small handful of parsley, leaves picked and
  finely chopped

METHOD

Cut eight slices of bread to the thickness of your little finger and toast (or griddle) on both sides. Once toasted, rub with the cut side of the garlic clove before drizzling a little olive oil over one side of each piece of bread.

Grate the tomatoes (using the coarse grating side of a box grater, or similar) into a small bowl. Season with the salt and leave to rest for a minute or so to release the juice from the tomatoes.

All that remains is to spoon the mixture over the bread, using the back of a spoon to rub the paste onto the bread. Scatter the parsley and drizzle with plenty more olive oil. Arrange on a serving plate.

Gazpacho
(Chilled tomato soup)

This is a simple recipe that relies on good-quality ingredients to create a final dish that will be an absolute joy. Serve cold for extra deliciousness.

Serves 4

INGREDIENTS

1 thick slice of stale white bread
400 g ripe tomatoes
1 red pepper
½ cucumber
1 garlic clove, peeled and minced
6 tbsp olive oil
1 tbsp red wine vinegar
½ tsp fine sea salt

METHOD

Place the bread in a shallow bowl and soak in two tablespoons of tap water.

Chop the tomatoes, deseed and chop the pepper and cucumber, and mince the garlic. Add these, along with the soaked bread, to a blender. Add the olive oil, vinegar and salt and blend to a smooth, soupy consistency.

If you need more water, add it a little at a time until you reach your desired consistency. Check and adjust the seasoning, then pass the soup through a fine sieve if you like a very smooth gazpacho.

Place in an airtight container in the fridge and chill for at least 2 hours before serving in little bowls.

Patatas bravas (Spicy potatoes)

Little cubes of fried potatoes topped with spicy tomato sauce is a sure-fire way to put a smile on anyone's face.

Serves 4–6

INGREDIENTS

1 litre sunflower oil, for frying
6 tbsp olive oil
2 garlic cloves, peeled and minced
400 g tin chopped tomatoes
1 red chilli, deseeded and finely chopped
2 tsp sweet smoked paprika
1 tsp fine sea salt
500 g potatoes, peeled and chopped into 3-cm (1-in.) chunks

METHOD

If you're a confident cook, heat the sunflower oil in a high-sided pan to 180°C (355°F). If not, preheat the oven to 200°C (400°F).

Meanwhile, combine the olive oil, garlic, tomatoes, chilli and paprika in a saucepan and bring to a boil over a medium heat. Simmer for 20 minutes, stirring occasionally, then season with the salt and set aside to cool.

Fry the potatoes in the hot oil until golden brown. If you'd rather roast the potatoes, place them in a roasting tray, toss with a little olive oil and some salt, and roast for 25–30 minutes, tossing halfway through, until golden brown.

To serve, plate up the cooked potatoes and cover in the spicy tomato sauce.

Croquetas (Croquettes)

Here follows a classic jamón croquetas recipe. If you fancy something different, substitute the jamón for the same quantity of whichever ingredient you prefer.

Serves 4

INGREDIENTS

25 g salted butter
2 tbsp olive oil
40 g plain flour
¼ tsp fine sea salt
½ nutmeg, grated
500 ml whole milk

100 g jamón, cut into
   0.5-cm (¼-in.) cubes
250 g breadcrumbs
2 eggs, beaten
2 tbsp milk
2 litres neutral oil
Lemon wedges,
   to serve

METHOD

In a large saucepan, melt the butter and olive oil over a medium heat until foaming. Add the flour and stir regularly for 5 minutes. Add the salt and nutmeg and stir to combine.

Start adding the milk, little by little, stirring to combine between each addition. Once all the milk is incorporated, reduce the heat and simmer for 4-6 minutes so that the roux thickens, stirring all the time.

Once nice and thick, stir in the jamón, then remove from the heat and set aside to cool completely.

Meanwhile, prepare your breading station: place the breadcrumbs in a wide tray, and whisk the eggs and milk together in a similar container. Using a wet spoon, scoop tablespoons of the croqueta mixture and form into neat round logs using your hands. Roll these in the breadcrumbs, then in the egg mixture, then back in the breadcrumbs. The double layer of crumbs will give you a lovely thick breaded crust.

Heat the neutral oil in a high-sided pan to 180°C (355°F) and fry the croquetas in batches of five or six for 3-4 minutes until dark golden brown. Place on kitchen paper, season with a little more salt and repeat until all the croquetas are cooked.

Serve while still warm with nothing more than a wedge or two of lemon.

Croquetas variations

Croquetas de bacalao: Made with bacalao (or whipped salt cod), these are the second best-loved croquetas in Spain.

Croquetas de boletus/champiñónes: Made with the earthy depth of good mushrooms.

Croquetas de cangrejo: These use delicious crab.

Croquetas de cecina: Made with *cecina de León* (or cured beef).

Croquetas de chorizo: These call for chorizo instead of jamón.

Croquetas de espinacas y queso: Made with spinach and cheese.

Croquetas de marisco: Made with seafood.

Croquetas de pollo: These contain pieces of chicken.

Croquetas de queso: Made with cheese.

WHAT KIND OF DOG ONLY EATS TAPAS? ESPAÑOL!

Tortilla (Spanish omelette)

This is a great vehicle for leftovers served with a green salad as a lunch or light supper. To serve as a tapa, cut into wedges and serve plain.

Serves 4

INGREDIENTS

4 tbsp olive oil
500 g potatoes, peeled and thinly sliced
1 white onion, peeled and finely sliced
1 tsp fine sea salt
5 medium eggs, whisked

METHOD

Heat two tablespoons of the olive oil in a frying pan (a 20-cm/8-in. pan works best) over a medium heat. Add the potatoes and cook, stirring frequently, for 5 minutes. Add the onion and salt and cook for a further 8–10 minutes, stirring regularly until the onion is soft and translucent but hasn't started to brown. If the onion is colouring at the edges, reduce the heat and continue cooking.

Add the remaining two tablespoons of olive oil and the whisked eggs to the pan, using a spoon to move everything about and help the egg settle in and around the potatoes and onion. Shake the pan gently a few times to make sure the egg is not sticking to the bottom of the pan.

Reduce the heat and let the omelette slowly set in the pan. When you can see the edges setting but the middle is still slightly loose, use a plate to turn out the tortilla before sliding it back into the pan to cook the other side. Cook for a few more minutes, using the time to tidy up the edges by gently pressing them down.

Once cooked, turn out onto a plate, cut into wedges and serve.

Calamares fritos (Fried squid)

Nothing beats a plate of freshly fried squid served alongside a bowl of garlicky aioli to dip it in.

Serves 4

INGREDIENTS

500 g fresh squid or frozen squid rings, defrosted
2 tbsp milk
4 tbsp cornflour
4 tbsp plain flour
1 tsp fine salt
1 litre sunflower oil
Lemon wedges and aioli, to serve

METHOD

If using fresh squid, wash the squid and remove the tentacles before cutting the main body into rings as thick as your little finger. Put into a bowl, stir in the milk and refrigerate for 30 minutes to a few hours.

Combine the flours and salt in a small bowl. Drain the squid well and pat dry with kitchen paper. Add the rings to the flour and toss so that they are well coated.

Heat the sunflower oil in a large saucepan over a medium heat to 180°C (355°F), or until a small piece of bread dropped into it sizzles immediately and goes golden brown in 20–30 seconds.

Fry the squid in batches for about 1 minute until crisp and golden brown. Drain on kitchen paper, sprinkle with salt, and serve with lemon wedges and aioli.

Gambas al ajillo (Garlic prawns)

This quintessential prawn dish has a real kick from the garlic and chilli, which is exactly what will keep you coming back for more.

Serves 4

INGREDIENTS

4 tbsp olive oil
4 garlic cloves, peeled and sliced
1 whole dried chilli, broken into 2–3 pieces
500 g raw prawns, peeled
Pinch of coarse sea salt
Bread, to serve

METHOD

Heat the olive oil in a frying pan over a medium heat. Fry the garlic and chilli until the garlic starts to brown at the edges and sticks together.

Stir in the prawns and salt, and cook until the prawns have turned pink all the way through.

Serve immediately with plenty of bread with which to soak up all the delicious juices.

Pulpo a la Gallega (Galician octopus)

Possibly the most famous tapa from Galicia. It's best if you can find pre-cooked octopus tentacles, but you can also cook them at home from raw.

Serves 4

INGREDIENTS

1 bay leaf
1 tsp fine sea salt
250 g octopus tentacles, cooked
2 tbsp olive oil
1 tbsp smoked paprika

METHOD

Add 500 ml of water, the bay leaf and salt to a saucepan to create a stock. Bring to a simmer over a medium heat. Add the octopus tentacles and simmer gently for 8–10 minutes to warm through.

Meanwhile, heat the olive oil in a frying pan, then remove from the heat and add the paprika, letting it sizzle a little as it cools down.

Once the octopus is cooked, remove from the stock and slice into 1 cm (¼ in.) thick rounds. Arrange on a plate and drizzle with the hot paprika oil and a pinch more salt.

Albóndigas (Meatballs)

Usually made with minced beef, pork or lamb, these little meatballs are a firm favourite with everyone, young or old.

Serves 4

INGREDIENTS

400 g beef, pork or lamb mince
(or a combination)

50 g breadcrumbs

1 garlic clove, peeled and grated

2 tsp sweet smoked paprika

1 egg, whisked

¾ tsp fine sea salt

1 tbsp olive oil

400 g tin chopped tomatoes

1 tbsp sherry vinegar

METHOD

In a bowl, combine the mince, breadcrumbs, garlic, paprika, egg and salt. Mix well to combine. Using wet hands, shape the mixture into 20 medium-sized balls.

Heat the olive oil in a large frying pan over medium-high heat, then fry the meatballs, turning every minute or so, until browned all over. Transfer to a plate and set aside, leaving the fat in the pan as this is the secret to getting as much flavour as possible into the final dish.

Add the tomatoes and sherry vinegar to the pan, bring to a boil, then add the meatballs and leave to bubble for 12 minutes on a low heat until the sauce thickens and the meatballs are completely cooked through.

Allow to cool a little before serving as one of a few tapas, or serve as a main meal with rice or potatoes and some greens or a salad.

Chorizo a la sidra or Chorizo al vino (Chorizo in cider or wine)

These are two firm favourites for any tapas aficionado. Rich, smoky and full of flavour from the chorizo, a little sharp and moreish from the cider or wine.

Serves 4

INGREDIENTS

1 tbsp olive oil
500 g fresh chorizo, sliced into
  2-cm (¾-in.) rounds
330 ml cider or red wine
2 bay leaves
Small bunch of parsley, roughly chopped

METHOD

Heat the olive oil in a frying pan over a medium heat. Add the chorizo and fry, tossing and turning occasionally, until it starts to brown.

Add the cider or red wine and the bay leaves, and toss the chorizo again to coat. Simmer for 6 minutes, or until the cider or wine is reduced by about half and starts to become a syrupy sauce. Add the parsley and immediately remove from the heat.

Spoon into a bowl and eat as part of a tapas spread or simply with a chunk of bread.

Conclusion

Two things should be clear by now: tapas are an essential part of Spanish culture, and are deeply ingrained in the country's social and culinary traditions.

From small cazuelas of patatas bravas to hearty plates of tortilla, they offer a visitor an achievable and delicious way to sample a broad variety of Spanish flavours and ingredients. And for the locals they are a way of life, part of the fabric of their day to day.

We have also learned that with tapas there are no rules. There are ubiquitous classics and unique regional specialities. Every possible element of the tapas experience could be different or exactly the same from place to place, tapa to tapa.

Armed with the key ingredients, techniques and classic tapas recipes, you can now bring Spanish culture into your kitchen. Don't be afraid to experiment.

Whether you're a novice in the kitchen or a keen chef, a foodie or just looking for a fun and casual dining experience, take everything you've learned here and share it with your family and friends. That is what tapas are all about, sharing little morsels of joy – so go forth and tapas!

Resources

BOOKS

Claudia Roden, *The Food of Spain* (2012)

Elizabeth Luard, *Tapas: Classic Small Dishes from Spain* (2017)

José Andrés, *The Book of Tapas* (2010)

Omar Allibhoy, *Tapas Revolution: 120 Simple Classic Spanish Recipes* (2013)

Ryland Peters & Small, *Tapas: and other Spanish plates to share* (2019)

WEBSITES

BBC Good Food

www.bbcgoodfood.com/recipes/collection/tapas-recipes

Brindisa Spanish Food

www.brindisa.com

***delicious.* magazine**

www.deliciousmagazine.co.uk/collections/tapas-recipes

Spanish Sabores

www.spanishsabores.com

Taste Atlas

www.tasteatlas.com

PODCASTS

The Spanish Food Cult

THE LITTLE BOOK OF SUSHI

Rufus Cavendish

Paperback

978-1-80007-840-6

From seaweed-wrapped maki rolls to tuna-topped nigiri, dive into this celebration of one of the world's favourite dishes. Including the history of sushi, a tour of its biggest names, delicious recipes and much more, *The Little Book of Sushi* will be your handy guide to the bite-sized delicacy that has found favour all over the world.

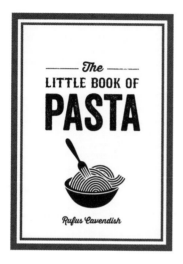

THE LITTLE BOOK OF PASTA

Rufus Cavendish

Paperback

978-1-80007-841-3

Whether fresh, dried, baked into lasagna or swirled as spaghetti around your fork, pasta is fantastic. From farfalle and fusilli to fettucine and beyond, this pocket guide serves up a celebration of one of the world's most popular foods. With history, trivia, tips and recipes, it's got all the information and inspiration you could hunger for.

Have you enjoyed this book?
If so, find us on Facebook at
SUMMERSDALE PUBLISHERS, on Twitter/X at
@SUMMERSDALE and on Instagram and TikTok at
@SUMMERSDALEBOOKS and get in touch.
We'd love to hear from you!

WWW.SUMMERSDALE.COM